STUDY GUIDE

The Book of Job

Derek W. H. Thomas

LIGONIER MINISTRIES

Renew your Mind.

LIGONIER.ORG | 800-435-4343

1

Job, Satan, & God

INTRODUCTION

The book of Job begins by introducing us to its three most significant characters: Job, Satan, and God. In this lesson, Dr. Thomas explores the difficulty of Job's suffering, Satan's involvement, and God's sovereignty.

LESSON OBJECTIVES

1. To introduce the book of Job and its primary characters
2. To introduce the nature of God's sovereignty over suffering

SCRIPTURE READING

There was a man in the land of Uz whose name was Job, and that man was blameless and upright, one who feared God and turned away from evil.

—Job 1:1

The LORD gave, and the LORD has taken away; blessed be the name of the LORD.

—Job 1:21

LECTURE OUTLINE

A. The book of Job revolves around the suffering of its protagonist—Job.
  1. Job was a historical person who was righteous and very blessed.
     a. He was from the land of Uz, lived at the time of Abraham, and is treated as a historical person in Ezekiel 14:14.
     b. He is declared "blameless and upright" three times in the opening chapters—once by the author and twice by God (Job 1:1, 1:8, 2:3).
     c. He was wealthy and had a wife and ten children.
  2. Job is presented as blameless and upright so that we know his suffering is not a punishment for some measure of ungodliness.

a. The book of Job asks difficult questions about the nature of suffering and God, such as, "Why are the godly permitted to suffer?"

b. The book of Job wrestles with the problem of evil and is considered a theodicy—a justification of the ways of God.

3. Job was innocent, though he was not sinless.

a. He is insistent that he is innocent and undeserving of punishment, but that does not mean Job was sinless.

b. There is no direct connection between any particular sin and his suffering, a principle also seen in John 9:1–3.

4. Job's innocence exacerbates the problem of suffering.

a. He seemingly loses everything in a single day, and his innocence only increases the difficulty of questions about suffering and God's sovereignty.

b. We can identify with Job in our own inexplicable sufferings, so it is no wonder that the Bible addresses these questions in one of the earliest canonical books.

B. The book of Job presents Satan as its central antagonist.

1. Satan is introduced very early but is not mentioned in Job's conversations with his friends and is only possibly alluded to by God in connection with Leviathan and Behemoth.

2. Satan is introduced as a drifter without a home who gives an account before God.

a. The fact that he must give an account to God shows that he is in no way equal with God.

b. Therefore, dualism is not a sufficient reason for suffering—there is not an equal power of good and evil at war in the universe.

3. Satan is directly connected to Job's suffering, but his involvement is not a sufficient explanation for Job's suffering.

a. God draws Satan's attention to Job, so God's sovereignty must be considered when we ask questions about suffering (Job 1:8).

b. God permits and restrains Satan to test Job, so Satan doesn't have ultimate control.

c. Nevertheless, Satan exists and is in direct opposition to God.

C. The book of Job is ultimately about God and His sovereignty over suffering.

1. God's sovereignty over suffering is the main concern of the book of Job.

a. Job forces us to ask the question, "Since God is all-powerful, why doesn't He prevent our suffering?"

b. C.S. Lewis calls this the problem of pain, and it can even be called the problem of God, but classically it is known as the problem of evil.

2. God's sovereignty is Job's comfort.

a. Job finds rest in the sovereignty of God: "The LORD gave, and the LORD has taken away; blessed be the name of the LORD" (Job 1:21).

      b. We can have rest, comfort, and peace by trusting in the sovereignty of God in the midst of our suffering.

  3. God's sovereignty isn't always easy to understand.

      a. Job will eventually begin to question God as the reality of his suffering becomes harsher and he descends into darker places.

      b. The circumstances of our own suffering can sometimes lead us to despair as we contemplate suffering's continual presence.

  4. God's sovereignty should be our comfort in the face of suffering.

      a. We should respond to suffering the way Job first responded to the calamity in his life, "Blessed be the name of the Lord" (Job 1:21).

      b. We must rest in His sovereignty, knowing His love and the reality that nothing ever happens to us outside of His gracious purposes.

STUDY QUESTIONS

1. Job is presented as sinless.
   a. True
   b. False

2. A _____ is a justification of the ways of God.
   a. Theocracy
   b. Theodicy
   c. Teleology
   d. Cosmology

3. Job was probably a contemporary of _____ .
   a. Abraham
   b. Jacob
   c. Moses
   d. David

4. Satan is a frequent character throughout the book of Job.
   a. True
   b. False

5. Job lost _____ children in one day.
   a. Two
   b. Four
   c. Eight
   d. Ten

6. C.S. Lewis called the tension created by the existence of suffering and the sovereignty of God the problem of _____ .
   a. Suffering
   b. Pain
   c. God
   d. Evil

DISCUSSION QUESTIONS

1. Why does suffering often make us question God's sovereignty?

2. Do you find God's sovereignty over suffering to be encouraging? Why or why not?

3. Job's initial response to his suffering was "The LORD gave, and the LORD has taken away; blessed be the name of the LORD" (Job 1:21). What do you find significant about Job's response?

4. How have you seen the graciousness of God work through your suffering?

2
Pain & Suffering

INTRODUCTION

God permitted Satan to attack Job's family and his wealth. Satan then set his aim on Job's health. In this lesson, Dr. Thomas engages with the difficult subject of pain and suffering in the life of the believer.

LESSON OBJECTIVES

1. To recount Job's faithfulness in the face of pain and suffering
2. To discuss the various attempts to solve the problem of pain and suffering

SCRIPTURE READING

Then Satan answered the Lord and said, "Skin for skin! All that a man has he will give for his life. But stretch out your hand and touch his bone and his flesh, and he will curse you to your face."

—Job 1:4

Count it all joy, my brothers, when you meet trials of various kinds.

—James 1:2

LECTURE OUTLINE

A. Satan appears before God to request permission to attack Job's health.
    1. Job did not curse God after Satan attacked his family and his wealth, so Satan returns in accusation that Job's afflictions were not enough.
        a. God presents Job as blameless and upright once again (Job 2:3).
        b. God permits Satan to attack Job's health but forbids him from taking Job's life (Job 2:4–6).
    2. God confirms the nature of Job's suffering.

        a.   The Hebrew word *hinnom* is used in Job 2:3 to imply that Satan instigated God to harm Job without reason.

        b.   God's providence is often difficult for us to understand, and the reasons behind it are not always apparent.

    3.   Satan inflicts Job with a disease that causes Job's body to waste away.

        a.   Throughout the book, Job's disease is described: he was covered with sores, lost his teeth, and his breath became putrid.

        b.   He scraped his skin with a piece of broken pottery for relief (Job 2:8).

B. Satan's attack of Job's health raises difficulties about the nature and reality of pain and suffering.

    1.   A cliché tells us, "If you have your health, you have everything."

        a.   This cliché is untrue and betrays a harmful philosophy that cannot comfort or console people who are sick and suffering.

        b.   This cliché can convey the idea that people who are sick and suffering have no hope and cannot be happy, which contradicts James 1:2.

    2.   Pain and suffering considered alongside the sovereignty of God raise questions about God's power or God's goodness.

        a.   A proper understanding of God's sovereignty views pain and suffering as part of His plan and purpose.

        b.   Improper understandings of God's sovereignty reject God's power, goodness, or the reality of pain and suffering itself.

    3.   Pain and suffering cause people to deny God's power.

        a.   Rabbi Harold Kushner's *When Bad Things Happen to Good People* suggests that God is not always powerful and in control.

        b.   The idea that God does not have total control suggests that we live in a dualistic universe of equal, opposing forces of good and evil.

    4.   Pain and suffering cause people to deny God's goodness.

        a.   God's sovereignty is maintained but God's goodness is denied in this solution to the problem of pain and suffering.

        b.   Islam's understanding of sovereignty with the horrors done in the name of Allah is an example of this deterministic worldview.

    5.   Pain and suffering even cause people to deny its reality.

        a.   Christian Science denies the reality of pain and suffering.

        b.   Christian Science teaches that pain and suffering are figments of our imagination.

    6.   Pain and suffering causes us to question God's willingness to heal.

        a.   Paul instructed Timothy to take wine for his stomach ailment (1 Tim. 5:23) and left Trophimus behind during a missionary journey because he was ill (2 Tim. 4:20).

        b.   Paul suffered from a thorn in the flesh that he prayed God would remove, and yet God did not remove it.

     c. Paul was an Apostle empowered with the gift of healing by the Holy Spirit, yet he was not able to heal these various ailments.

     d. God does not always heal our pain and suffering, but his power is made perfect in our weakness (2 Cor. 12:9).

C. Job remains steadfast despite his wife's counsel.

   1. Job's wife is introduced and says to Job, "Curse God and die."

     a. Augustine referred to Job's wife as *diaboli adiutrix*—the devil's advocate.

     b. Calvin referred to Job's wife as *organum satani*—the tool of the devil.

   2. Job's wife could be interpreted differently.

     a. She has also suffered the loss of her ten children.

     b. She may not want to see Job in pain any longer.

   3. Job does not curse God, declaring, "Shall we receive good from God, and shall we not receive evil?" (Job 2:10).

     a. Job acknowledges the foolishness of his wife's speaking as if God didn't exist (Ps. 14:1).

     b. Job's declaration is an affirmation of God's sovereignty.

   4. God is in ultimate control.

     a. God is not the author of evil, but He is in control, allowing things to fall out by secondary causes.

     b. Our confidence is in our good, powerful, and sovereign God, who works all things together for good for those who love Him (Rom. 8:28).

STUDY QUESTIONS

   1. Most commentators sympathize with Job's wife.

     a. True

     b. False

   2. Rabbi Harold Kushner's *When Bad Things Happen to Good People* suggests that God is not always powerful and in complete control.

     a. True

     b. False

   3. A _____ universe has equal, opposing forces of good and evil.

     a. Monistic

     b. Dualistic

     c. Animistic

     d. Pluralistic

   4. The thorn in Paul's flesh could probably be related to his eyesight.

     a. True

     b. False

5. Goodness is a subcategory in the doctrine of God in _____ .
    a. Islam
    b. Judaism
    c. Hinduism
    d. Christianity

6. Calvin used the Latin term *organum satani* to refer to _____ .
    a. Job
    b. Satan
    c. Job's wife
    d. Job's children

DISCUSSION QUESTIONS

1. What is a proper way to understand pain and suffering in the providence of God? How should this understanding change the way we respond to pain and suffering?

2. How would you console someone in the midst of pain and suffering using the truth of God's sovereignty?

3. Denying God's power, denying His goodness, or denying the existence of pain and suffering are offered as solutions to the problem of evil. Why are each of these options dangerous?

4. How would you explain the fact that though God is sovereign, He is not the author of sin?

3

The Dark Night of the Soul

INTRODUCTION

The third chapter of the book of Job is one of the darkest chapters in the Bible. In the midst of his suffering, Job begins to curse the day he was born. In this lesson, Dr. Thomas explores the dark imagery Job uses to describe his suffering and how we are to understand it as Christians.

LESSON OBJECTIVES

1. To explain Job's shocking expressions of lament
2. To encourage appropriate ways of reading one of the darkest chapters in the Bible

SCRIPTURE READING

After this Job opened his mouth and cursed the day of his birth.

—Job 3:1

All Scripture is breathed out by God and profitable for teaching, for reproof, for correction, and for training in righteousness.

—2 Timothy 3:16

LECTURE OUTLINE

A. The third chapter of the book of Job is one of the darkest chapters in the Bible.

1. Job begins to curse the day he was born.
   a. The opening verse sets the tone for a chapter full of graphic illustrations expressing the nature of Job's desperation.
   b. Job's use of the word "darkness" evokes Psalm 88: "My companions have become darkness."
2. The prophet Jeremiah quotes from the third chapter of Job after spending a night in prison, as though this was a passage he had memorized (Jer. 20:14).
3. Job's lament suggests that he believes the peace and presence of God that often accompanies trials has fled him, contemplating only his suffering.

4. The background of Job's suffering must be considered before we can pass judgment on Job's lament.
    a. A considerable amount of time has passed since Job's initial loss, and time has affected his mood and perspective.
    b. Job's friends had arrived to accompany Job, but they are silent and their actions suggest that they expect Job will die (Job 2:11–13).
    c. Job may have begun to contemplate his wife's words, "Curse God and die" (Job 2:9).
    d. God has been silent, making no attempt to comfort Job.
5. Job's expressions of lament are shocking and graphic.
    a. He curses the day he was born, wishing he had been stillborn or had died in infancy.
    b. He alludes to Leviathan, the chaos monster of destruction and evil mentioned in Job 38–40.
6. Job's expressions of lament are manifestations of a nihilistic cynicism.
    a. Job had begun to doubt that life had any meaning or purpose.
    b. C.S. Lewis was tempted to such cynicism after the death of his wife.

B. How should Christians understand the third chapter of the book of Job?
1. The third chapter of the book of Job is part of the inerrant Word of God.
    a. "All Scripture is breathed out by God" (2 Tim. 3:16–17).
    b. As part of the inerrant Word of God, it teaches us something about the nature of suffering and comforts those in times of despair.
2. The third chapter of the book of Job teaches us to be sensitive to Christians who experience great amounts of pain and suffering.
3. The third chapter of the book of Job highlights the fact that God does not immediately appear to reprimand Job.
    a. Job's lament goes too far, but we should sympathize with him and understand the difficulty of navigating God's relationship to suffering.
    b. God is compassionate, and Jesus Christ felt this desperation in the garden of Gethsemane.
4. The third chapter of the book of Job reminds us that "we do not have a high priest who is unable to sympathize with our weaknesses" (Heb. 4:15).
    a. Jesus Christ knew what it was to be forsaken by God in ways that we will never experience (Matt. 27:46).
    b. We must take comfort knowing that Jesus Christ sympathizes with us in our suffering.

STUDY QUESTIONS

1. Job's lament is a reaction to the commentary of his friends.
    a. True
    b. False

2. The prophet _____ quotes from the third chapter of Job with familiarity.
    a. Isaiah
    b. Daniel
    c. Ezekiel
    d. Jeremiah

3. Job makes a reference to _____ during his lament.
    a. Molech
    b. Ashtoreth
    c. Behemoth
    d. Leviathan

4. Job's lament proves that he is an unbeliever.
    a. True
    b. False

5. "_____ has become my companion" (Ps. 88:18) is a summary of Job's lament.
    a. Trial
    b. Death
    c. Trouble
    d. Darkness

6. The third chapter of Job is *theopneustos*, "_____."
    a. God-sent
    b. God-given
    c. God-breathed
    d. God-delivered

DISCUSSION QUESTIONS

1. Could someone use the third chapter of Job appropriately to justify desperate feelings about the futility of life? Why or why not?

2. Considering the context of Job's lament, why should we sympathize with his suffering?

3. Why do you think C.S. Lewis said it would be more dangerous to believe false things about God than to disbelieve in God?

4. What events in Christ's life help us to see that He is sympathetic to us in our weaknesses?

4

Miserable Comforters

INTRODUCTION

Eliphaz is the first of Job's friends to speak, but like all of Job's friends, he is a miserable comforter. In this lesson, Dr. Thomas explores Job's dialogue with Eliphaz and explains his improper use of the principle of repercussion.

LESSON OBJECTIVES

1. To reiterate Job's innocence in the face of his suffering
2. To clarify how a principle of repercussion is valid and biblical but not always applicable

SCRIPTURE READING

Those who plow iniquity and sow trouble reap the same.

—Job 4:8b

Jesus answered, "It was not that this man sinned, or his parents, but that the works of God might be displayed in him."

—John 9:3

LECTURE OUTLINE

A. Eliphaz believes Job is suffering as a repercussion of his sin.

1. The dialogue between Job and his friends begins in the fourth chapter of the book of Job.
   a. Eliphaz is the first to speak, probably because is the eldest; he has grey hair, and he is older than Job's father (Job 15:9–10).
   b. Eliphaz's speeches are lengthy, and he claims to have received his message from God.

2. Eliphaz believes that Job is reaping what he has sown (Job 4:7–8; 5:6–7).
    a. Eliphaz is certain that the universe operates mechanically on a principle of justice such that you always reap what you sow.
    b. Eliphaz believes Job's suffering is a consequence of his actions, that there is a sin in Job's life that has brought this calamity upon him.

B. Eliphaz is partly right, because actions do have consequences.
    1. "Do not be deceived: God is not mocked, for whatever one sows, that will he also reap" (Gal. 6:7).
    2. God's wrath is present in the universe as a consequence of sin; it is the reflex of His holiness toward sin (Rom. 1:18–32).
    3. Uzzah was struck dead because he placed his hand on the ark of the covenant (2 Sam. 6:5–15).
        a. The ark of the covenant represented the presence of God, and God demanded that it be handled accordingly.
        b. The Philistines captured the ark of the covenant, and it was placed on an ox cart on the way back to Jerusalem after it was reclaimed.
        c. The ark was to be carried by its poles and never to be touched (Num. 4:15).
        d. Apart from a biblical worldview with a robust understanding of God's holiness, it is hard to explain how Uzzah reaped what he had sown.
    4. Ananias and Sapphira were struck dead because they lied to the Holy Spirit.
        a. Ananias sold his property and withheld a portion of the proceeds from the church in the full knowledge of his wife, Sapphira.
        b. Ananias and Sapphira lied to the church that existed within the living memory of Pentecost with manifestations of Apostolic gifts.
        c. Like Uzzah when he touched the ark of the covenant, Ananias and Sapphira were an affront to the presence and holiness of God.
        d. They lied to God the Holy Spirit, and they reaped what they sowed.
    5. Some Corinthians became weak and ill and some even died because they would not partake of the Lord's Supper in a worthy manner (1 Cor. 11:17–34).
    6. So why did Jesus die?
        a. One possible answer: Justice doesn't exist, because Jesus didn't deserve to die.
        b. The correct answer: Jesus did deserve to die, because He was reckoned to be sin on our behalf (2 Cor. 5:21).

C. Eliphaz is partly wrong, because suffering is not always a consequence of sin.
    1. The disciples asked Jesus about the man born blind, "Rabbi, who sinned, this man or his parents, that he was born blind?" (John 9:2).
        a. The presumption behind the disciples' question was that the man's blindness must be the result of sin and God's judgment upon it.
        b. Jesus answered that there was not a direct connection between the man's blindness and a sin committed by him or his parents.

    c.   Jesus answered further that the man was blind so that Jesus might display the works of God through healing him.

    d.   God used this man's suffering in order to teach and educate others.

  2. Paul asked three times for the thorn in his flesh to be removed, yet there is no indication that it was a punishment from God (2 Cor. 12:1–10).

  3. God disciplines those whom He loves (Heb. 12:6).

D. Job responds to Eliphaz's accusations of guilt (Job 6–7).

  1. Job declares that Eliphaz is overconfident, longwinded, and more like a storm that comes and goes than a comforting friend.

  2. Job's final words in response say in effect, "You're going to miss me when I'm gone."

  3. Eliphaz has a simplistic view of suffering as a punishment for some known or unknown sin, and he is partially right.

  4. Eliphaz does not take into account the complexity of life and the reality that suffering is not always a direct result of something we have done.

E. The dialogue between Job and Eliphaz teaches two very important lessons.

  1. Well-intentioned counselors can be wrong.

  2. God's thoughts are not our thoughts, and God's ways are not our ways.

STUDY QUESTIONS

1. Eliphaz's worldview revolves around cosmic justice.
    a. True
    b. False

2. Eliphaz believes that suffering is _____.
    a. Tragic
    b. Illusory
    c. Punishment
    d. Unexplainable

3. _____ was struck dead after touching the ark of the covenant.
    a. Ahio
    b. Uzzah
    c. Samuel
    d. Abinadab

4. The man in the ninth chapter of John was born blind because of the sin of his parents.
    a. True
    b. False

5. _____ wrote that Jesus was "the greatest sinner the world has ever seen."
   a. Calvin
   b. Luther
   c. Aquinas
   d. Augustine

6. Understanding _____ is critical to understanding the punishment of Christ on the cross.
   a. Election
   b. Adoption
   c. Imputation
   d. Sanctification

DISCUSSION QUESTIONS

1. In what ways was Eliphaz right? In what ways was he wrong?

2. Why are the stories of Uzzah and Ananias and Sapphira difficult for people to understand apart from a biblical worldview?

3. If the wages of sin is death, and Jesus never sinned, then why did He die?

4. Has your suffering ever been used by God as an example in someone else's life? Has someone else's suffering ever been used by God as an example in your own life?

5

Contending with God

INTRODUCTION

Bildad the Shuhite is the next of Job's friends to speak, but like Eliphaz before him, his understanding of justice causes him to wrongly doubt Job's innocence. In this lesson, Dr. Thomas discusses the impossibility of contending with God.

LESSON OBJECTIVES

1. To introduce the second of Job's miserable comforters
2. To clarify Job's desire for someone to plead his case before God

SCRIPTURE READING

Does God pervert justice? Or does the Almighty pervert the right?

—Job 8:3

But how can a man be in the right before God?

—Job 9:2

LECTURE OUTLINE

A. Bildad the Shuhite is next in the line of Job's miserable comforters, espousing the same worldview as Eliphaz and questioning Job's innocence.

1. Bildad the Shuhite begins by asking the question, "Does God pervert justice?"
   a. Bildad shares the same worldview as Eliphaz where the world operates on a strict principle of justice.
   b. Bildad and Eliphaz rightly believe in the law, justice, and God's sovereignty, but they misapply these truths.
2. Bildad asserts that if Job is innocent then God will restore him (Job 8:6).
   a. He believes that God's judgment can only be explained by Job's sin, so Job should not expect God to pervert justice.

      b. He considers the fact that God hasn't yet restored Job to be evidence that Job is not innocent.

      c. He is certain that Job must be wrong, because he views all suffering as a form of divine retribution.

B. Job maintains his innocence and laments, "There is no arbiter between us."

    1. Job 9:33 can be translated in different ways.

      a. It can be translated to express a wish: "Would that there were an arbiter between us."

      b. It can be translated to express a fact: "There is no arbiter between us."

    2. Job's desire for an arbiter allows us to imagine Job pleading his case before God, feeling alone with no one to represent him.

      a. He is wrestling with the questions "Is God good?" and "Is God good toward me?"

      b. He believes in the sovereignty and the justice of God, but he is being tempted to doubt if God can be trusted.

    3. Job understands the futility of contending with God, the futility of attempting to be in the right before Him.

      a. Job 9:2 does not primarily concern Job's sin, because Job still maintains his innocence—in fact, we were told he was innocent.

      b. Job 9:2 concerns justice with God, because Job believes that he's suffering unjustly, and there is no higher court of appeal than God.

      c. Job knows that he cannot make an argument before God and needs to appeal for mercy.

      d. Job distrusts that God would even hear him, and even if God were to reply, he "could not answer him once in a thousand times" (Job 9:3).

    4. Job's statements make it clear that he believes in a powerful and sovereign God who cannot be questioned (Job 9:4–12).

    5. Job's statements about "the bowed helpers of Rahab" (Job 9:13) do not mean that Job believed in ancient Near Eastern creation myths.

    6. Job begins to lament his life, because he feels the weight of his cynicism as he questions whether or not God's ways are arbitrary (Job 9:20–21).

C. Job has an arbiter in Jesus Christ.

    1. Job is not asking for someone to forgive his sins but is rather asking for someone to plead his case before God.

    2. Jesus Christ is a Savior who not only forgives sin but also heals broken hearts; He knows injustice firsthand—He is our advocate (1 John 2:1).

STUDY QUESTIONS

    1. Bildad and Eliphaz have different understandings of justice.

      a. True

      b. False

2. _____ said, "Job's friends have a very bad case, but they argue it extremely well. Job has a very good case, and he argues it very badly."
   a. Lewis
   b. Luther
   c. Calvin
   d. Augustine

3. "There is no arbiter between us" (Job 9:33), a statement of fact, can be translated alternatively as a statement of _____ .
   a. Alarm
   b. Desire
   c. Dismay
   d. Expectation

4. Job is wrestling with the question "Can I trust God?"
   a. True
   b. False

5. Job mentions "the helpers of _____," an allusion to an ancient Near Eastern creation myth.
   a. Enki
   b. Apzu
   c. Rahab
   d. Marduk

6. Bildad believes that suffering is instant retribution without _____ .
   a. End
   b. Cause
   c. Meaning
   d. Exception

DISCUSSION QUESTIONS

1. Why are Job's friends such miserable comforters?

2. What doctrines can help in warding off doubts and desperation similar to those that Job is feeling?

3. Job replied to Bildad, "How can a man be in the right before God?" How is Job's meaning different from the meaning of the well-known verse "None is righteous, no, not one" (Rom. 3:10)?

4. How is Jesus Christ not only an advocate for us when we sin but also an advocate for us while we suffer?

6

My Redeemer Lives

INTRODUCTION

"For I know that my Redeemer lives" are perhaps the most well-known, hope-filled words in all the book of Job. In this lesson, Dr. Thomas examines this glimpse of Job's faith and his continued belief in the justice of God and the resurrection to come.

LESSON OBJECTIVES

1. To define what Job means by "Redeemer"
2. To recount Job's faith in the justice of God despite his suffering
3. To explore Job's statement about the bodily resurrection of the dead

SCRIPTURE READING

For I know that my Redeemer lives.

—Job 19:25a

Thus says the Lord, the King of Israel, and his Redeemer, the Lord of host: "I am the first and I am the last; besides me there is no god."

—Isaiah 44:6

LECTURE OUTLINE

A. Job has been pleading his case with God, declaring his need for an arbiter, his hope for a witness in heaven, and, suddenly, his confidence in his Redeemer.

   1. Job has been calling out to God for justice. Since God has not answered, Job has begun to question whether or not He is even listening.
   2. Job had mentioned his need for an arbiter who would stand before God and his witness in heaven who would testify for him in heaven (Job 9:33; 16:19).
   3. Suddenly, Job mentions his steadfast confidence in a Redeemer (Job 19:25).

      a. The silence of God up to this point magnifies the suddenness of Job's statement, "For I know that my Redeemer lives."

      b. The light that shines in the darkness of Job's suffering is the work of the Holy Spirit.

B. Job proclaims his belief in a redeemer who will plead his case before God.

    1. The word "redeemer" is the Hebrew word *goel*.

    2. The word "redeemer" is used in the story of Ruth, Naomi, and Boaz.

      a. While in Moab, Naomi suffered the loss of her husband and two sons who had married Moabite women.

      b. One of Naomi's daughters-in-law, Ruth, vowed to follow Naomi to Bethlehem and worship the God of Israel.

      c. Naomi had a kinsmen redeemer in Bethlehem, a brother of her husband, who was under legal obligation to her as a widow.

      d. Boaz married Ruth and became Naomi's kinsmen redeemer.

    3. The word "redeemer" must be understood in the same sense as in the story of Ruth, Naomi, and Boaz.

      a. Job is not speaking of a redeemer who will forgive his sins, because Job is suffering innocently.

      b. Job is speaking of a redeemer who will legally defend him before God.

C. Job is responding to Bildad the Shuhite's monologue in the eighteenth chapter, which can be called "The Dwelling Places of the Wicked."

    1. "The Dwelling Places of the Wicked" is Bildad's illustration of an old man stumbling along a path falling down over every obstacle in his way.

      a. Bildad is using the illustration as a picture of God's punishment of the wicked, a life full of unexpected calamity and terror.

      b. Bildad plays on words with the common name for a Canaanite god, *Mot*, and the Hebrew word for "death."

    2. "The Dwelling Places of the Wicked" is Bildad's illustration for Job.

      a. Bildad mentions sulfur, which is scattered over dead bodies, in reference to Job's ten children (Job 19:15).

      b. Bildad purposefully notes that there is no one left to succeed Job after his fast-approaching death—no one to remember him.

D. Job's response to Bildad the Shuhite's monologue culminates in his statement, "For I know that my Redeemer lives" (Job 19:25).

    1. Job feels that God and his own counselors have rejected him.

      a. Job gives voice to the agony caused by the words of his friends who take his insistence personally, not as a plea to God (Job 19:5–6).

      b. Job knows that he is innocent and has a deep sense of injustice, but everyone is driven away by his misery (Job 19:13–22).

      c. Job appears to be in jeopardy of disbelieving in justice entirely.

    2. Job suddenly announces, "For I know that my Redeemer lives."

a. Job anticipates that there will be someone who will be obligated to plead and defend his case.

b. Job's belief that his rights will ultimately be honored demonstrates that he believes that we live in an ordered universe.

3. Job believes in the physical resurrection of the dead (Job 19:25–27).

a. Some commentators believe that Job is merely embodying his case and testifying to his continued belief that justice will prevail.

b. Job's language is too strong for such an interpretation: "In my flesh I will see God" (Job 19:25–27).

4. Job's belief in a physical resurrection is a God-given belief.

a. Job's belief cannot be explained from the surrounding ancient world or, because it is such an early book, from other biblical texts.

b. God gave Job a moment of insight and faith in the midst of his sorrow.

5. Job understands that he may die without justice, yet he holds fast to the integrity of the justice of God.

a. God's justice is a great comfort for those who may never see the wrongs done against them made right.

b. Jesus Christ is our Redeemer who will defend and plead our case before Almighty God.

STUDY QUESTIONS

1. Some commentators argue that Job doesn't actually believe in the bodily resurrection of the dead.

    a. True

    b. False

2. *Goel* is the Hebrew word for "_____."

    a. Death

    b. Arbiter

    c. Witness

    d. Redeemer

3. _____ preached the sermon Dr. Thomas named "The Dwelling Places of the Wicked."

    a. Elihu

    b. Bildad

    c. Zophar

    d. Eliphaz

4. The illustrations in "The Dwelling Places of the Wicked" are intended to parallel the circumstances of Job's suffering.

    a. True

    b. False

5. The book of _____ helpfully clarifies what Job means by "redeemer."
   a. Joel
   b. Ezra
   c. Ruth
   d. Esther

6. There is a play on words in "The Dwelling Places of the Wicked" using the Hebrew word for "death" and one of the Canaanite gods, _____ .
   a. Mot
   b. Baal
   c. Dagon
   d. Moloch

DISCUSSION QUESTIONS

1. What are some contributing factors to Job's growing sense of injustice?

2. In what ways does Job's understanding of the word "redeemer" differ from the ways we commonly understand it?

3. Describe the illustration used in "The Dwelling Places of the Wicked." How is it intended to be representative of Job's suffering?

4. How would you argue that Job's statement about the resurrection is not merely a literary technique but a confirmation of his belief in the bodily resurrection of the dead?

7

The Wisdom of God

INTRODUCTION

The perplexing reality of pain and suffering makes us ask the question, "Where can wisdom be found?" In this lesson, Dr. Thomas recounts Job's asking this question and his answer, "in the Lord."

LESSON OBJECTIVES

1. To define wisdom according to a biblical worldview
2. To analyze the competing worldviews that masquerade as wisdom
3. To resolve the problem of pain and suffering in the wisdom of God

SCRIPTURE READING

From where, then, does wisdom come?

—Job 28:20a

God understands the way to it, and he knows its place.

—Job 28:23

And he said to man, "Behold, the fear of the Lord, that is wisdom, and to turn away from evil is understanding."

—Job 28:28

LECTURE OUTLINE

A. The book of Job is fundamentally about wisdom.
    1. The twenty-eighth chapter of the book of Job is a speech about wisdom.
        a. Job is responding to the short speech given by Bildad—the shortest speech given by any of Job's friends (Job 25).

b. It is similar to other portions of wisdom literature found in the Bible, such as Ecclesiastes and Proverbs.

c. There is an epistemological battle raging in the book of Job in which Job is searching for a metanarrative to explain everything.

2. Wisdom is the power to see and the inclination to choose the best and highest goal with the surest means of attaining it.

B. Science and philosophy compete with the biblical worldview to give an answer as to where wisdom can be found.

1. Science attempts to find wisdom through man's exploration of the world.

a. Job describes man as an explorer who mines for precious resources in the depths of the earth, yet cannot find wisdom (Job 28:1–11).

b. Similarly, scientific theories attempt to discover the origins of the universe, erroneously positing that something came from nothing.

2. Philosophy attempts to find wisdom through questioning basic assumptions about the nature of reality.

a. John Cage, a twentieth-century composer, created a silent piece of music as a postmodern attack against the idea of metanarratives.

b. Eastern mysticism posits the existences of an abstract, ambiguous force balancing the universe.

c. Epicureanism denies the biblical metanarrative in favor of pleasure-fueled materialist philosophy.

d. Secular humanism fails to give any explanations for the unspeakable tragedies that occur and offers no solace to those afflicted by them.

3. The outcome of searching for wisdom apart from God is meaninglessness.

a. Death often causes us to question whether life has any meaning.

b. In Ecclesiastes, the Preacher wrestles with the question of life's meaning, even to the extent of declaring our vaporous life a vanity.

c. Job's cynicism about whether life has any meaning can be heard in Job 7:17–19.

C. Job maintains his beliefs despite his encroaching cynicism.

1. Job continues to argue that he hasn't committed any particular sin that warrants the visitation of God's judgment as manifested in his trials.

a. Job holds onto the fact that he is the man of integrity testified about in the opening chapters by God (Job 27:6).

b. Job does not concede to the arguments of his friends that suffering is always a form of retribution.

2. Job's encroaching cynicism has led him to dwell on the question of where wisdom can be found, and he rightly concludes that it is found in God.

a. Job compares man's search for wisdom as a mining expedition; the most valued resources known to man cannot buy it (Job 27:12–19).

b. The metanarrative within the book of Job that explains the problem of pain and suffering is the wisdom of God.

STUDY QUESTIONS

1. Wisdom is the power to see and the inclination to choose the best and highest goal with the surest means of attaining it.
   a. True
   b. False

2. _____ gives the shortest speech of all of Job's friends.
   a. Elihu
   b. Bildad
   c. Zophar
   d. Eliphaz

3. "Gather ye _____ while ye may" is the first line of a poem by Robert Herrick that portrays a cynical outlook on the meaning of life.
   a. Lovers
   b. Flowers
   c. Trophies
   d. Rosebuds

4. A metanarrative is an explanation of everything.
   a. True
   b. False

5. *Qoheleth* is the Hebrew word for the Preacher in the book of _____ .
   a. Proverbs
   b. Psalms
   c. Ecclesiastes
   d. Lamentations

6. Samuel Friedman wrote, "In a crisis, the humanists seem _____ ."
   a. Absent
   b. Hopeful
   c. Heartbroken
   d. Courageous

DISCUSSION QUESTIONS

1. Why do you think John Cage's composition *4'33"* is a postmodern attack on metanarratives?

2. Why doesn't the humanist message help in times of tragedy? How does the biblical message give hope?

3. What is the significance of Job's illustration of man's search for wisdom as a mining expedition?

4. In seasons of pain and suffering, where do we often search for wisdom apart from God?

8

The Sovereignty of God

INTRODUCTION

Elihu is introduced after Eliphaz, Bildad, and Zophar have long concluded that Job's suffering must be a punishment for sin. In this lesson, Dr. Thomas looks at Elihu's contribution to the book of Job and what it teaches about the sovereignty of God.

LESSON OBJECTIVES

1. To evaluate Elihu's perspective of suffering as a means of instruction
2. To discover the implications of God's sovereignty in our pain and suffering

SCRIPTURE READING

Whether for correction or for his land or for his love, he causes it to happen. Hear this, O Job; stop and consider the wondrous works of God.

—Job 37:13–14

LECTURE OUTLINE

A. Elihu contributes a new perspective on the problem of Job's suffering.
1. Elihu is introduced after Job's friends have ceased to answer Job, concluding that Job was righteous in his own eyes.
   a. He has been present and listening to all of Job's speeches and those of Job's friends.
   b. He is angry that Job justified himself rather than God and that Job's three friends could not answer him (Job 32:2–3).
2. Commentators are divided about Elihu.
   a. Some commentators believe that Elihu is repeating the argument that suffering is a form of retribution.
   b. Calvin believed that Elihu was advancing a new argument and that it answered the problem of pain and suffering.

    c. Elihu introduces a new line of argumentation, but he slowly digresses into the same argument that Job's three friends have been making.

3. Elihu rightly asserts that the answer to the problem of pain and suffering cannot be at the expense of God's character (Job 34:12).

    a. The righteousness and the goodness of God must be maintained in any proposed solution to the problem of pain and suffering.

    b. Islam offers a solution to the problem of pain and suffering that maintains God's sovereignty at the expense of God's goodness.

4. Elihu believes that instruction is the purpose of suffering.

    a. He believes that suffering is intended to teach us something about God and something about ourselves.

    b. In all of Job's protests and assertions of his rights as innocent, Job's sinful character has emerged, which supports Elihu's belief.

    c. Sin can manifest itself in the course of a trial, even if it wasn't the cause of the trial.

5. We must not respond to suffering by bringing accusations against God.

    a. If we respond to suffering by questioning, accusing, or asserting our rights before God, we have forgotten that God created us.

    b. Christ called us to take up our cross and follow Him; we don't assert our rights and privileges in cross bearing, so we shouldn't in suffering.

6. Elihu believes that suffering can lead us to a greater appreciation of God's mercy, for God disciplines those whom He loves (Heb. 12:3–11).

B. Elihu reiterates the perspective of Job's friends in his emphasis on the sovereignty and power of God.

1. Elihu stresses the sovereignty and power of God because he believes that Job has protested only in the interest of self-justification.

    a. Self-justification is our natural tendency in pain and suffering.

    b. Self-justification ceases as pain and suffering begin to teach us that we are in the hands of a sovereign, omnipotent, almighty God.

2. Job believes in the sovereignty of God, but has failed to see the implications of the sovereignty of God in his suffering.

    a. God is sovereign, so we don't have a right to know all the answers as to why we are suffering.

    b. God is sovereign, so we must depend on Him for knowledge in order to understand our suffering.

3. Elihu's arrogant disposition has been present in his argument, nonetheless he does teach us something right about suffering as a means of instruction.

STUDY QUESTIONS

1. Elihu is angry that Job's friends have not attempted to defend Job.

    a. True

    b. False

2. _____ believed that Elihu provided an answer to the problem of pain and suffering.
   a. Calvin
   b. Luther
   c. Aquinas
   d. Augustine

3. Elihu gives _____ speeches in the book of Job.
   a. One
   b. Two
   c. Three
   d. Four

4. The answer to the problem of pain and suffering cannot be at the expense of the character of God.
   a. True
   b. False

5. Elihu's agitation with Job is similar to Gertrude's sentiment in *Hamlet*, "The lady doth _____ too much."
   a. Permit
   b. Protest
   c. Profess
   d. Proclaim

6. Elihu reiterates that God opens the _____ of men by adversity.
   a. Ears
   b. Eyes
   c. Hands
   d. Hearts

DISCUSSION QUESTIONS

1. What is Elihu's answer to the problem of suffering? Is his position valid in comparison to the position of Job's friends?

2. What are the implications of God's sovereignty for how we ought to react in times of pain and suffering?

3. How does Christ's command that we take up our cross and follow Him inform how we ought to face pain and suffering?

4. How do seasons of pain, suffering, trials, and temptation reveal ways in which we need to repent?

9

Out of the Whirlwind

INTRODUCTION

Finally, God speaks, answering Job out of the whirlwind with a lengthy sequence of questions that reveal to Job the true nature of his complaint. In this lesson, Dr. Thomas explains what these questions reveal about God and man.

LESSON OBJECTIVES

1.   To explore the content of God's questions to Job
2.   To discover the purpose of God's questions to Job

SCRIPTURE READING

Then the Lord answered Job out of the whirlwind and said: "Who is this that darkens counsel by words without knowledge?"

—Job 38:1–2

"Behold, I am of small account; what shall I answer you?"

—Job 40:4a

LECTURE OUTLINE

A. God challenges Job after Elihu's speech on the majesty of God.

1. Elihu's speeches are intended to draw our attention to the sovereignty and majesty of God.

   a. Commentators are divided as to whether God approves of Elihu's speeches because God is silent about the issue.

   b. Some believe that God's silence is an approval, and others believe that God's silence is a condemnation.

   c. The majesty of God is a vital part of the way in which trials and suffering teach us.

2. God issues a challenge to Job for speaking without knowledge.
   a. God challenges Job to "dress for action," a verb that relates to wrestling in the Hebrew.
   b. God responds to Job's questions with questions, which shows that the contest between God and Job is not a contest of equals.

B. God's questions are intended to create a contrast between God and man.
   1. Job has been seeking an explanation for his suffering and has been asserting his right for an answer, so God questions the true extent of his knowledge.
   2. God asks more than fifty questions that silence Job in order to exalt His majesty.
      a. He questions Job about creation and the order of the universe.
      b. We should be filled with amazement as we consider His wisdom in creation and the limited extent of our knowledge.
   3. God created us as creatures who gain knowledge, wisdom, and understanding of His world.
      a. We have been created in God's image and mandated to subdue the earth.
      b. We cannot fulfill the creation mandate without knowledge of God's universe, so we are by nature explorers.
      c. Nonetheless, there are many things we cannot know.
   4. God's questions exalt His majesty, providing Job with proper perspective.
      a. Job has blamed God for his suffering because he has not been given an answer as to why he is suffering.
      b. God's questions reveal to Job how much he would need to know to understand his suffering because of the interrelatedness of the world.
      c. God has ordered the end from the beginning and so has perfect knowledge; His questions help Job to see that he is not God.
   5. The majesty of God helps Job to understand how small he is as a creature.
      a. The contrast created by God's questions and Job's inability to answer them reminds Job that he is small in comparison to God' majesty.
      b. We are image bearers of God, and Jesus was sent to redeem us, but we must always remember that we are His creatures.
   6. God graciously humbled Job (Job 40:3–5).

STUDY QUESTIONS

1. God's silence concerning Elihu's speech is a clear condemnation of Elihu.
   a. True
   b. False

2. Herman Bavinck said, "_____ is the vital element of dogmatics."
   a. Faith
   b. Truth
   c. Reason
   d. Mystery

3. The verb "dress for action" is used in relation to _____ in Hebrew.
    a. Sparring
    b. Running
    c. Wrestling
    d. Exploring

4. Our mandate from God to subdue the earth is a reason for exploration and scientific discovery.
    a. True
    b. False

5. God asks Job _____ to _____ questions to convey His majesty.
    a. 10; 20
    b. 20; 30
    c. 40; 50
    d. 50; 60

6. God mentioned Pleiades and _____ as He questioned Job.
    a. Vela
    b. Orion
    c. Aquila
    d. Cepheus

DISCUSSION QUESTIONS

1. In what ways has your own suffering highlighted the contrast between who you are and who God is?

2. How does the creation mandate to subdue the earth help us to understand more about ourselves as God's creatures?

3. What parts of God's creation move you the most to think about His grandeur and majesty?

4. Why does God answer Job with a series of questions? What does God's line of questioning reveal about the relationship between them?

10

Behemoth & Leviathan

INTRODUCTION

God challenges Job a second time by directing his thought to consider Behemoth and Leviathan. In this lesson, Dr. Thomas seeks to help us identify Behemoth and Leviathan and understand why they are relevant to Job's suffering.

LESSON OBJECTIVES

1. To understand what is meant by Behemoth and Leviathan
2. To determine Behemoth and Leviathan's relevance to Job's sufferings

SCRIPTURE READING

Behold, Behemoth, which I made as I made you.

—Job 40:15a

O Lord, how manifold are your works! In wisdom have you made them all; the earth is full of you creatures. Here is the sea great and wide, which teems with creatures innumerable, living things both small and great. There go the ships, and Leviathan, which you formed to play in it.

—Psalm 104:24–26

LECTURE OUTLINE

A. God speaks to Job a second time to teach Job about His nature and character.

1. God speaks to Job out of the whirlwind, which conveys the reality that God does not always answer us in ways we would expect.
2. God introduces Behemoth and Leviathan in order to instruct Job, because thus far, God has only silenced him.

B. Behemoth and Leviathan can be interpreted in various ways.

1. Behemoth is a land creature, and Leviathan is a sea creature.

    a. Behemoth means "beast," which is plural in Hebrew, so it is the intensification of the idea of a beast.

    b. Leviathan is a sea monster, which in the Greek Septuagint is translated as "dragon."

2. Some interpreters believe that Behemoth and Leviathan were dinosaurs whose extinction can be explained by catastrophism, i.e., the global flood.

3. Some interpreters believe Behemoth and Leviathan are actual creatures.

    a. Behemoth was understood as an elephant or a hippopotamus in the English literature of the Renaissance and post-Renaissance period.

    b. Likewise, Leviathan is identified as a crocodile.

4. Some interpreters believe Behemoth and Leviathan are demonic.

    a. The interpretation of Behemoth and Leviathan as demonic stems from the use of such animals in ancient Near Eastern literature.

    b. This interpretation gives demonic activity a significant role in the suffering in the world.

    c. Satan did play some role in Job's suffering, but it is doubtful that Job would have interpreted Behemoth and Leviathan as demonic.

C. God introduces Behemoth and Leviathan so that Job will learn to trust Him.

1. Behemoth and Leviathan are relevant to the problem of pain and suffering.

    a. Derek Kidner points out in his commentary on Job that only God knows why He created the hippopotamus and the crocodile.

    b. We may not know why God permits us to suffer, but we can be sure that God knows why He permits us to suffer.

2. God will be glorified by the pain and suffering that exists in this world.

    a. God created the hippopotamus and the crocodile for His glory, and God will also be glorified by pain and suffering.

    b. God demonstrated His love and mercy and was glorified by the pain and suffering of Jesus Christ on our behalf.

    c. God has used pain and suffering in His definite plan for our salvation, so we can be sure that He is in control of our suffering (Acts 2:23).

3. Behemoth and Leviathan could possibly be mythological creatures.

    a. Behemoth and Leviathan could have been significant creatures in the ancient Near East.

    b. Behemoth and Leviathan could be used to show that the mythological creatures conceived in ancient times are nothing compared to God.

4. God uses Behemoth and Leviathan to teach Job how to exercise faith in Him.

    a. Job does not understand the nature of his suffering, but he must have faith that God understands and is in control of his suffering.

    b. God does not merely leave Job silent but brings him to a place where he can confess, exercise faith, and bow down before Him.

5. God works all things together for good (Rom. 8:28).
   a. God is not the author of sin; we can trust Him.
   b. God sent His Son into the world for us, and if we can trust Him with our sin, we can trust Him in our suffering.

STUDY QUESTIONS

1. The movement to identify Behemoth and Leviathan with actual creatures occurred during the Reformation.
   a. True
   b. False

2. The Greek Septuagint translates Leviathan as "_____."
   a. Snake
   b. Dragon
   c. Monster
   d. Crocodile

3. Behemoth can be literally translated to mean "_____."
   a. Beast
   b. Elephant
   c. Brontosaurus
   d. Hippopotamus

4. The origin of sin lies outside of the direct causation of God.
   a. True
   b. False

5. Interpreters believe that Behemoth and Leviathan are _____.
   a. Demonic
   b. Dinosaurs
   c. Mythological
   d. All of the above

6. The belief that our fossil records and the extinction of species are the result of the global flood is called _____.
   a. Gradualism
   b. Creationism
   c. Catastrophism
   d. Uniformitarianism

DISCUSSION QUESTIONS

1. Of the different views people have taken on Behemoth and Leviathan, which view do you think is the most convincing? Why?

2. How are Behemoth and Leviathan relevant to the problem of pain and suffering?

3. What does the fact that Jesus Christ suffered for us reveal about the nature of pain and suffering?

4. God spoke to Job a second time, so that Job would not be left in silence with his hands over his mouth. In what ways does this reveal the love of God to those who are suffering?

11

Repentance & Restoration

INTRODUCTION

The book of Job ends on a positive note of repentance and restoration. In this lesson, Dr. Thomas discusses the significance of Job's deeper relationship with God, the reconciliation with his friends, and the enjoyment of his renewed life.

LESSON OBJECTIVES

1. To highlight significant themes in the last chapter of the book of Job
2. To reiterate the importance of trusting God through pain and suffering

SCRIPTURE READING

I had heard of you by the hearing of the ear, but now my eye sees you; therefore I despise myself, and repent in dust and ashes.

—Job 42:5–6

And the LORD restored the fortunes of Job, when he had prayed for his friends. And the LORD gave Job twice as much as he had before.

—Job 42:10

LECTURE OUTLINE

A. Job repents of his sin, and God restores him.
    1. The book of Job does not end on a tragic note.
        a. Job repents of his sin in dust and ashes (Job 42:1–6).
        b. God restores to Job his fortune, family, and friendships (Job 42:7–17).
    2. Job repents of the sin he had committed over the course of his trial.
        a. Job is not repenting of the sin that his friends had assumed was the cause of his trial; Job has been vindicated before his friends.

      b. Job is repenting of his attitude toward God that he had expressed over the course of his trial.

B. Job develops a richer relationship with God as a result of his trial.

    1. Job understands more about the majesty and incomprehensibility of God.

    2. Job has been brought to dependence on and faith in God.

    3. Tragedies can bring us from the early stages of acceptance through the uncertainty caused by our grief to a deeper relationship with God.

        a. William Cowper, a famous hymn writer and friend of John Newton, struggled with suicidal depression. He grew closer to God as a result.

        b. Marriages built on gospel foundations can survive through periods of trial to develop into deeper relationships marked by affection and love.

        c. Trials can help our relationship with God as we are led to depend on Him in ways we wouldn't have otherwise.

C. Job is reconciled with his friends as a result of his trial.

    1. Job is contrasted with his three friends (Job 42:7).

        a. God commends Job's confession and repentance.

        b. God condemns Job's friends for their misrepresentation of Him.

    2. The wrath of God is a reality.

        a. C.H. Dodd did not believe in the subjective anger of God but rather that anger was an objective and abstract reality of our fallen universe.

        b. True biblical counseling must be undertaken in all seriousness, which requires an acknowledgment of God's anger.

    3. God is angry with Job's friends for their misrepresenting Him and for their lack of compassion toward Job.

    4. Job offers sacrifices and prays for his friends.

        a. Job's friends bring him seven bulls and seven rams as part of their confession and reconciliation to Job.

        b. Job, a contemporary of Abraham, precedes the Levitical priesthood in interceding on his friend's behalf.

        c. Job is Christlike in his willingness to forgive his repentant friends, and likewise we need to be willing to forgive those who are repentant.

    5. Forgiveness is essential to move beyond the pain caused to us by others.

        a. Trials can make us bitter and, as such, are a threat to our well-being if we are not able to forgive others and move forward in a biblical way.

        b. When God forgives our sins, He forgets them; He doesn't keep a record to remind us of our sins against Him (1 Cor. 13:4–7).

D. Job experiences a renewed life as the result of his trial.

    1. The book of Job ends in a wonderful way: "And the Lord blessed the latter days of Job more than his beginning" (Job 42:12).

    2. Job is blessed with ten children—seven sons and three daughters.

        a. Job names his daughters Jemimah, Keziah, and Keren-happuch.

      b. Jemimah means "dove"; Keziah means "cinnamon"; Keren-happuch means "container of antimony," an eye shadow.

  3. Job is a testimony that God can radically change circumstances.

      a. Job must not be used as an example to prove that trials always result in greater blessing.

      b. Job should be used as an example to prove that it is possible for God to radically change circumstances.

STUDY QUESTIONS

1. After Job's trials, he was blessed with _____ children.
   a. Three
   b. Seven
   c. Ten
   d. Twelve

2. John Newton's friend and fellow hymn writer _____ struggled with suicidal depression, out of which grew a deeper relationship with God.
   a. Isaac Watts
   b. Horatius Bonar
   c. Charles Wesley
   d. William Cowper

3. The New Testament scholar _____ did not believe in the wrath of God.
   a. C.H. Dodd
   b. A.A. Hodge
   c. B.B. Warfield
   d. F.F. Bruce

4. Job made sacrifices for his friends as a Levitical priest.
   a. True
   b. False

5. The number of bulls and rams Job sacrifices is _____ .
   a. Three
   b. Six
   c. Seven
   d. Twelve

6. Job names one of his daughters _____, which means "dove."
   a. Yonah
   b. Keziah
   c. Jemimah
   d. Keren-happuch

DISCUSSION QUESTIONS

1. How can the transformation of Job's attitude encourage us in times of difficulty?

2. Is it dangerous to ignore or downplay God's righteous wrath, especially as we consider God's character? Why or why not?

3. How is Job's sacrifice and prayer for his friends a lesson to us for how we are to handle reconciliation with others?

4. How would you graciously respond to a friend who appeals to the last chapter of the book of Job for the guarantee of blessing after a season of difficulty and suffering?

12

The Patience of Job

INTRODUCTION

James presents Job as a prime example of patience in the face of pain and suffering. In this lesson, Dr. Thomas clarifies what James means by "the steadfastness of Job" by highlighting all of the ways Job has been faithful in his suffering.

LESSON OBJECTIVES

1. To explain what James means by "the steadfastness of Job"
2. To demonstrate the steadfastness of Job in the face of pain and suffering

SCRIPTURE READING

You have heard of the steadfastness of Job, and you have seen the purpose of the Lord, how the Lord is compassionate and merciful.

—James 5:10–11

LECTURE OUTLINE

A. James uses Job as an example of patience in suffering.
    1. Suffering is a major theme in the book of James.
        a. The book of James begins and ends with the theme of suffering (James 1:2, 5:7–12).
        b. James presents the prophets as examples of those who have been steadfast in suffering, but he appeals specifically to Job.
    2. James' emphasis on Job's steadfastness is warranted.
        a. Our first impulse is to question whether Job is the best example of steadfastness.
        b. Job seems to have lost patience with his friends and with God, but Job persevered through the darkest hours of his life.

B. Job is steadfast in affirming the sovereignty of God.

   1. Job may have begun to question God's love, but he never questioned the sovereignty of God.

   2. Job understood that nothing happens outside of God's decree.

      a. The Westminster Confession of Faith uses the language of first and secondary causes, echoing the thought of the Reformers and medieval theologians concerning God's sovereignty.

      b. God established secondary causes, but they fall out according to His eternal decree—nothing takes God by surprise.

      c. The only basis upon which we can say God works all things together for our good is God's sovereignty.

   3. The sovereignty of God is a central theme in the book of Job.

      a. The book of Job could not be a theodicy if the sovereignty of God were not a central theme.

      b. The relationship of evil to an omnipotent and loving God would not be a problem apart from Job's steadfast belief in God's sovereignty.

C. Job is steadfast in his faith in God.

   1. Job directs his questions and even his anger toward God, which shows that even in his darkest moments, his belief in God never wavered.

   2. A hymn by John Newton summarizes Job's trial and the deeper relationship he would come to have with God as a result.

      a. Our prayers for greater faith and maturity in the Christian life are often answered in unexpected ways.

      b. God may allow difficult situations to increase our dependence on Him as a way of answering our prayer.

   3. Job may not have all the answers as to why he was permitted to suffer, but he has learned to trust God in the midst of his trials.

D. Job is steadfast in assessing himself in the light of God's sovereignty.

   1. Job learned not to be surprised by God.

      a. A professing Christian may dismiss the idea that pain and suffering will inevitably be a reality in his life, but Job learned otherwise.

      b. Job discovered that he was created by God and that he had no right to an explanation for his suffering.

   2. Job learned to express his steadfastness in the words of Isaiah and Moses.

      a. "For as the heavens are higher than the earth, so are my ways higher than your ways and my thoughts than your thoughts" (Isa. 55:9).

      b. "The secret things belong to the Lord our God, but the things that are revealed belong to us and to our children" (Deut. 29:29).

3. Job never learned about Satan.
   a. Satan is not a prevalent figure in the Old Testament, but just as he would personally attack Jesus Christ, Satan personally attacked Job.
   b. Job remained steadfast despite Satan's best attempts.
   c. Job did not succumb to the temptation to curse God.
   d. Job's steadfastness is a great encouragement to all believers because it demonstrates God's promises to keep and protect us.

E. What does James mean by the steadfastness of Job?
   1. James is drawing our attention to the possibility of surviving a trial of the magnitude of Job's trial.
      a. Job survives and flourishes after his trial.
      b. Not all trials end beautifully, but we can rest assured that we will find joy with God in heaven and that God will keep us until we arrive.

STUDY QUESTIONS

1. The emphasis on God's sovereign, eternal decree was the unique development of the Westminster Confession of Faith.
   a. True
   b. False

2. James specifically names _____ as an example of steadfastness.
   a. Job
   b. Hosea
   c. Ezekiel
   d. All of the above

3. Dr. Thomas used a hymn by _____ as a summary of the book of Job.
   a. Isaac Watts
   b. John Newton
   c. Horatius Bonar
   d. William Cowper

4. Job ultimately learns about Satan's role in his suffering.
   a. True
   b. False

5. According to Dr. Thomas, Satan is a prevalent figure in the Old Testament.
   a. True
   b. False

6. _____ had an utterly unique relationship with God and yet said, "The secret things belong to the Lord our God."
   a. Job
   b. David
   c. Isaiah
   d. Moses

DISCUSSION QUESTIONS

1. How does Dr. Thomas highlight Job's steadfastness despite his seeming impatience with God and his three friends?

2. John Newton wrote a hymn about how God answered his prayer for increased faith by bringing about difficult circumstances. Considering Job, in what ways do difficult circumstances serve as fertile soil for God to increase our faith in Him?

3. We are largely unaware of the opposition that faces us as Christians. In what ways can we understand Satan's personal attack against Job as an encouragement rather than a discouragement?

4. How does the revealed will of God give us comfort despite His secret will's remaining hidden?

ANSWER KEY FOR STUDY QUESTIONS

Lesson 1
1. B
2. B
3. A
4. B
5. D
6. B

Lesson 2
1. B
2. A
3. B
4. A
5. A
6. C

Lesson 3
1. B
2. D
3. D
4. B
5. D
6. C

Lesson 4
1. A
2. C
3. B
4. B
5. B
6. C

Lesson 5
1. B
2. C
3. B
4. A
5. C
6. D

Lesson 6
1. A
2. D
3. B
4. A
5. C
6. A

Lesson 7
1. A
2. B
3. D
4. A
5. C
6. A

Lesson 8
1. B
2. A
3. D
4. A
5. B
6. A

Lesson 9
1. B
2. D
3. C
4. A
5. D
6. B

Lesson 10
1. B
2. B
3. A
4. A
5. D
6. C

Lesson 11
1. C
2. D
3. A
4. B
5. C
6. C

Lesson 12
1. B
2. A
3. B
4. B
5. B
6. D